The
SCHOOL
GOVERNOR'S
& PARENT'S
Handbook

The SCHOOL GOVERNOR'S & PARENT'S *Handbook*

Lawrie Baker

foulsham

LONDON • NEW YORK • TORONTO • SYDNEY

foulsham

Yeovil Road, Slough, Berkshire SL1 4JH

ISBN 0–572–01558–5

Copyright © 1990 Lawrie Baker

Printed in Great Britain at St Edmundsbury Press
Bury St Edmunds

ACKNOWLEDGEMENTS

I wish to acknowledge the help and support of colleagues at the National Foundation for Educational Research, with both the preparation and content of this handbook. I should also like to thank: –

1. Lancashire County Council, for the use of their sample budgets and chart of procedures for the exclusion of a pupil.

2. Industry Matters, for the use of their diagram of Pupil Support, taken from their "Information Pack for School Governors from the Business Community".

LWB

CONTENTS

INTRODUCTION

This book is written firstly for governors, but it should also be helpful to all interested parents.

No doubt you are a busy person with a life of your own to lead, so you may not have time to read this handbook from cover to cover. Don't worry, you don't need to. It has been prepared to give you guidance and information *when you need it*. It is divided into sections so that you can refer easily to the topic which concerns you. It also has an index and a glossary of educational terms at the back.

One cautionary note:
Remember this handbook is a governors' guide and not a statement of education law. For that you need to refer to the text of the various Education Acts.

To be an effective governor there is a lot to learn and a lot to do. This handbook is intended to help by giving you some background knowledge, but information alone will not make you a successful governor. This can only come about when you play an active part in the governing body and take a keen interest in the school you serve.

You will also soon recognise the importance of a strong partnership between the school, the governing body and the local education authority.

Whatever the work and responsibilities may be, above all, enjoy being a governor.

1
THE EDUCATION
SERVICE

The four principal partners in the education system are:—

1. CENTRAL GOVERNMENT

      – Department of Education and Science (DES)
      – Secretary of State for Education and Science

   ROLE – To provide legislative framework for the education system
      – To ensure LEAs provide facilities and services
      – To control expenditure, building programmes
      – To provide political direction to the system.

The headquarters of the DES is in London at Elizabeth House, York Road, near Waterloo Station. It has a staff of about 2,000 civil servants. It is responsible for, among other things, maintaining national educational standards. In this it is assisted by Her Majesty's Inspectorate (HMI). There are about 450 HMI in England and over 40 in Wales.

2. LOCAL EDUCATION AUTHORITIES (LEAs)

      – County Councils, Metropolitan District Councils, London Boroughs.

ROLE – To decide local budgets and priorities
 – To decide local education pattern – age ranges
   of schools, etc.
 – To oversee curriculum and other policies

There are at present 96 LEAs in England. The Inner London Education Authority, (to be disbanded in 1990 when its responsibilities will be taken over by the 13 Inner London boroughs), 20 Outer London Boroughs, 36 Metropolitan Districts and 39 Counties. There are 8 LEAs in Wales – all Counties.

Each LEA is required to appoint an Education Committee which consists mostly of members elected to the County, District or Borough Council, though almost all include in addition some members co-opted for their knowledge and experience of education. Each Authority is obliged to appoint a Chief Education Officer (or Director) who is assisted by a Deputy, by Assistant Education Officers and by Local Advisers or Inspectors.

3.   GOVERNING BODIES

ROLE – To manage individual schools: buildings, policies, finance, curriculum
 – To select staff.

4.   HEADTEACHERS AND STAFF

ROLE – To run schools on a day-to-day basis.

2
TYPES OF SCHOOLS AND GOVERNING BODIES

Schools in England are either "maintained" or "independent". "Independent" schools receive most of their income from fees and are virtually free from government control. "Maintained" schools have their running costs met by local education authorities and provide free education. Two-thirds of the maintained schools ("county schools") are run entirely by local education authorities. The remaining third are "voluntary schools" in which another body (e.g. the Roman Catholic Church) has an interest. The voluntary schools are mostly of two kinds: "aided" and "controlled".

1.   COUNTY SCHOOLS

- Primary, secondary and special schools in which no denominational religious teaching is given
- Entirely maintained by LEA
- Teachers employed by LEA
- Teachers and parents elected as Governors

2. VOLUNTARY CONTROLLLED SCHOOLS

  - Halfway between county and aided
  - All running/building costs paid by LEA
  - Teachers employed by LEA
  - Denominational teaching can be given (for not more than 2 periods a week)
  - Teachers and parents elected as Governors
    (The voluntary body appoints a minority of governors)

3. VOLUNTARY AIDED SCHOOLS owned by voluntary body (e.g. Church)

  - Running expenses paid by LEA, number of staff decided by LEA
  - Building costs – 15% borne by church/foundation, 85% by DES
  - Staff appointed and employed by Governors
  - Governing bodies – mostly appointed by church/foundation
  - Denominational teaching allowed
  - Teachers and parents elected as Governors

4. HOSPITAL SCHOOLS

  Hospital authorities can arrange with LEAs for the use of the hospital premises as special schools.

5. GRANT MAINTAINED SCHOOLS

  Any county or voluntary school with more than 300 pupils may apply to the Secretary of State for grant-maintained status. A formal application will need the support of a majority of parents voting in a secret ballot. The school must retain the same character after the change as before and will not be able to charge fees.

6. CITY TECHNOLOGY COLLEGES

The Secretary of State may enter into agreements with any persons wishing to set up a City Technology College (CTC) which:

a) is in an urban area

b) provides education free of charge for pupils of different abilities aged 11–19 from the local community

and c) has a broad curriculum with emphasis on science and technology.

PATTERN OF ORGANISATION OF SCHOOLS

This varies widely between and sometimes within LEAs. The reasons for the variations may be historical, or to do with the availability of accommodation at different levels, but the main reason is often the LEA's philosophy about whether it is better to transfer children at 11+, 12+ or 13+.

YOU WILL NEED TO FIND OUT WHAT THE PATTERN IS IN YOUR LEA.

Some primary schools cater for the complete primary range (5–11). Others provide for part of the range:
Infant schools (5–7) are linked to Junior schools (7–11)
First schools (5–8 or 5–9) are linked to Middle schools (8–12 or 9–13)

The most common overall patterns are these:—

TWO-TIER SYSTEM

Primary school 5–11
Secondary school 11–18

This retains the traditional age of transfer at 11.

THREE-TIER SYSTEM WITH MIDDLE SCHOOLS

First school 5–8 or 9
Middle school 8 or 9 — 12 or 13
Upper school 12 or 13 — 18.

In a few cases the First and Middle Schools may be combined.

THREE-TIER SYSTEM WITH BREAK AT 16

Primary school 5–11/12
Secondary school 11/12–16
Sixth form or tertiary college for 16+

PRE-SCHOOL EDUCATION

By law, children must be admitted to full-time education by the school term following their 5th birthday.

Many receive some education at an earlier age in local authority or private nursery provision or in the reception class of a primary school.

3
THE LOCAL EDUCATION AUTHORITY

The organisation of education at local level is the responsibility of the local education authority (LEA).

THE EDUCATION COMMITTEE

The LEA is required by law to set up an education committee. This normally consists of:

Elected members (Councillors)
Additional members (usually people with a special interest in education) plus representatives of the churches

EDUCATION SUB-COMMITTEES

The Education Committee delegates many of its decision-making powers to sub-committees. These vary in name and number from LEA to LEA. There may be separate sub-committees for schools, further education, development, finance, policy, general purposes, staffing etc.

You will need to find out what sub-committees there are in your LEA.

Most members of the sub-committees may also be school governors, so one or two may be on your school governing body.

Resolutions passed by your governing body are usually presented to the next meeting of the appropriate sub-committee for comment or action.

THE EDUCATION SERVICE

The Education Commitee delegates the day-to-day running of the service to the Chief Education Officer or Director of Education, whose Department provides the necessary administrative and professional support. The staff of the Department are Local Government Officers who carry out the policy of the Education Committee.

Governors will often hear the Education Department referred to as "The Office".

In large LEAs there will often be more than one Education Office. In large counties there will be the main office – County or Shire Hall – and Area Offices. In a Metropolitan Authority (e.g. Manchester, Birmingham) there may be a Central Office and District or Divisional Offices.

4
THE GOVERNING BODY

1. Governing bodies are set up under two legal documents, The Instrument of Government and the Articles of Government. These are based on guidelines and models provided by the Secretary of State for Education and Science and have to comply with the law as it now stands.

   The 1986 Education Act required LEAs to make new Instruments and Articles for all county, voluntary and maintained special schools.

The Instrument of Government lays down the rules for meetings and who is on the Governing Body.

The Articles of Government deal with the duties, powers and responsibilities of governors.

All members of the Governing Body and every teacher at the school must be given a free copy of the Instrument and Articles of the school.

2.   Formal meetings of the Governing Body must be held at least once every school term.

In addition, AT THE REQUEST OF ANY THREE GOVERNORS the Clerk must call a special meeting of the Governing Body to discuss any specific issue. Except in cases of extreme urgency due notice of such a meeting must be given. (Consult the Instrument of Government.)

Decisions cannot be taken at a meeting unless a minimum number of governors is present. This is called a quorum. The minimum number is normally three governors or one third of the complete membership rounded up to a whole number.

Remember, all governors are equal

3.   The governors present at the meeting will include:

a) Local Authority representatives – these will be nominated by the LEA and will include at least one councillor

b) Parents – elected by parents of the school

c) Teachers – elected by the staff

d) People from the community and industry – chosen by the rest of the Governing Body

e) The headteacher – who may choose whether or not to be a governor and is usually present.

f) (In **voluntary schools**) Foundation governors – see page 20–1.

4.   Governors hold office for a four-year term and can be re-elected or re-appointed for a further term.
Parent Governors whose children leave the school may complete their term of office.
Teacher governors, however, must give up their governorship when they leave the school, as must the headteacher.

5.   Governors may not hold governorships of more than four schools.

6.   Governors who, without the consent of the Governing Body, fail to attend meetings for twelve months are disqualified.

7.   The composition of governing bodies is set down in the 1986 Education Act:—

County and voluntary controlled schools

Up to 99 pupils
 	
2 parents
2 LEA appointees
1 teacher
3 co-optees
   (or 1 co-optee +
   2 foundation
   governors* at
   controlled schools)
1 headteacher
   (if head so chooses)
	100-299 pupils
	
	3 parents
	3 LEA appointees
	1 teacher
	4 co-optees
	   (or 1 co-optee +
	   3 foundation
	   governors* at
	   controlled schools)
	1 headteacher
	   (if head so chooses)

300-599 pupils
 	
4 parents
4 LEA appointees
2 teachers
5 co-optees
   (or 1 co-optee +
   4 foundation
   governors* at
   controlled schools)
1 headteacher
   (if head so chooses)
	600 + pupils**
	
	5 parents
	5 LEA appointees
	2 teachers
	6 co-optees
	   (or 2 co-optees +
	   4 foundation
	   governors* at
	   controlled schools)
	1 head teacher
	   (if head so chooses)

* foundation governors at controlled schools are appointed to represent the interest of the Church authority or voluntary organisation which provides the school.

** these schools have the option of adopting the composition specified for schools of 300–599 pupils.

Voluntary aided and special agreement schools (see glossary)

The composition of the governing bodies of these schools was not changed by the Act. The non-foundation governors must comprise:

— at least one parent
— at least one LEA appointee
— at least one teacher for schools with 299 or fewer pupils and at least two teachers for larger schools
— at least one minor authority appointee at primary schools serving an area with a minor authority (e.g. a Parish Council)
— the headteacher if he or she so chooses
— sufficient foundation governors (one of whom must be a parent) to outnumber the others by two if the governing body has 18 or fewer members and by three if it is larger.

Grant-maintained schools

— Five parent governors
— At least one but not more than two teacher governors
— The person who is for the time being the Headteacher
— A sufficient number of first governors (in the case of ex-county schools) or foundation governors (in the case of ex-voluntary schools) to outnumber the other governors. At least two of these must be parents of registered pupils when they take office.
— The Secretary of State has the power to appoint two additional governors if the existing governors are not carrying out their duties adequately.

8. Three people have particular roles at the governors' meeting:

a) The Clerk or Secretary to the Governors

b) The Chair

c) The Headteacher

The Clerk or Secretary is appointed in order:

To draft and type the agenda after approval from the Chair

To collect the relevant documents together and send them to governors before each meeting

To attend the meeting, take notes and compile and re-prograph the minutes after the meeting, writing any follow-up letters as requested by the Chair

The Chair is elected by the Governors annually, together with the Vice-Chair.

It is the Chair's job to ensure agenda items are properly discussed and decisions are made in an effective and sensible way.

In addition to their role in meetings, Chairs of governors have other duties concerning the day-to-day running of the school. Many meet the Head on a regular basis to keep abreast of the schools' activities and discuss problems as they arise. They also have a key role in the appointment of staff.

In general, they may act on behalf of the Governing Body in any urgent matter at any time. But their action is then a personal one, and assumes the Chair has the confidence of the Governing Body. To be effective and legitimate, personal actions taken by the Chair must be expressed as a formal decision of the next governors' meeting.

The Headteacher attends each meeting whether a governor or not and makes a report. He or she will:

Consult governors about what is taught in the school

Seek their help and advice in certain matters

Keep them informed of school progress, problems and activities

Contribute expertise to discussion and decision-making

Exercise certain powers delegated by the Governing Body (e.g. capitation – see page 28)

5

THE MAIN RESPONSIBILITIES OF THE GOVERNING BODY

The responsibilities of the governing body are set out in detail in the Articles of Government of each school.

In general, however, these responsibilities are for:

1. FINANCE

2. THE CURRICULUM

3. PUPILS

4. STAFFING

5. PREMISES

6. ANNUAL REPORT AND PARENTS' MEETING

The 1988 Education Act gave greatly increased powers to the governing bodies at those schools which will be operating under a scheme for Local Management of Schools (LMS). These changes are described in detail under Finance (p.28) and Staffing (p.44) and in the relevant sections of the summary of the 1988 Education Act.

1. FINANCE

All expenditure on schools (except for 'unofficial funds' – see page 28) is financed through either 'revenue' or 'capital'. The basic difference between revenue and capital expenditure is that revenue is paid for out of the Council's current income i.e. the community charge, whereas capital is paid by taking out loans which are repaid over a number of years. The interest on these loans is charged to revenue.

A. NON-LMS SCHOOLS

1. School Expenditure/Costs

Under the 1986 Education Act the Governing Body must receive from the LEA an annual statement of the cost of running the school. This will show how money has been spent on such items as staff, fuel, furniture, cleaning, caretaking, examination fees, telephones, travelling expenses, etc. It will also show the money that has been received from such things as lettings, examination fees, private telephone calls, etc. This statement is provided to help the Governors decide whether the money has been used economically, efficiently and effectively.

Here are two sample balance sheets, one for a primary and one for a secondary school:

25

SAMPLE A

County Primary School
Expenditure and Income – Financial Year April to April

Expenditure	£	£
Employees		
Teaching staff	88,387	
Caretaking and Cleaning Staff	8,583	
Other Non-teaching Staff	4,585	101,155
Premises		
Maintenance of Buildings	7,373	
Fuel, Light, Water & Cleaning Materials	6,465	
Furniture & Fittings	272	
Rent & Rates	1,156	15,266
Supplies & Services		
School Allowance	2,990	
Cleaning and Domestic Supplies	55	
Examination Fees	0	3,045
Other Expenditure		
Travelling & Subsistence Expenses	95	
Telephones	280	
Other Expenses	0	375
TOTAL EXPENDITURE		119,841
Income		
Sales/Private Telephone Calls	0	
Examination Fees	0	
Rents/Lettings	0	
Miscellaneous Income	186	
TOTAL INCOME		186
TOTAL NET EXPENDITURE		119,655

SAMPLE B

County Secondary School
Expenditure and Income – Financial Year April to April

Expenditure	£	£
Employees		
Teaching Staff	711,727	
Caretaking & Cleaning Staff	37,043	
Other Non-teaching Staff	32,949	781,719
Premises		
Maintenance of Buildings	61,226	
Fuel,Light, Water &		
Cleaning Materials	27,994	
Furniture & Fittings	1,509	
Rent & Rates	47,519	138,248
Supplies & Services		
School Allowance	39,302	
Cleaning & Domestic Supplies	954	
Examination Fees	11,596	51,852
Other Expenditure		
Travelling & Subsistence		
Expenses	1,288	
Telephones	2,909	
Other Expenses	0	4,197
TOTAL EXPENDITURE		976,016
Income		
Sales/Private Telephone Calls	68	
Examination Fees	737	
Rents/Lettings	36	
Miscellaneous Income	30	
TOTAL INCOME		871
TOTAL NET EXPENDITURE		975,145

2. Capitation/School Allowance

Under the 1986 Education Act the LEA has a duty to make available annually to the Governing Body a sum of money to be spent under the direction of the Governors on books, equipment, stationery, etc. This is called the capitation or school allowance. The Governing Body may delegate the spending of this money to the Head.

The capitation, or school allowance, is financed from revenue and is calculated on the number and ages of the children in the school.

3. Unofficial Funds

Whenever a school earns money through its own efforts, (e.g. concerts, fairs) or receives donations, this money is put into an unofficial fund. The Governing Body must make sure this money is properly handled, and give details of any donations the school has received in its annual report to parents.

B. LOCAL MANAGEMENT OF SCHOOLS

The 1988 Education Act devolves greater financial and organisational powers to governing bodies, adding to those responsibilities already given them by the 1986 Act.

Under the new system, the LEA must determine each year:
- The amount of money it needs to keep centrally for such things as capital expenditure (including structural maintenance) central administration, inspectors, educational psychologists and contingencies
- The amount of money it will make available overall for schools
- How it is going to share this money out fairly among the schools

This sharing out must be done by means of a formula which allows, first and foremost, for differences in the numbers and ages of pupils. Schemes must then be submitted by the LEAs to the Secretary of State for approval.

Under the new system of Local Management of Schools, once the total sum to be allocated to a particular school has been settled by the LEA, it will be up to that school to organise its own budget. Local Management of Schools will be brought in gradually but it is likely that all secondary schools and the bigger primary schools (over 200 pupils) will have responsibility for their own budgets by 1991.

The school will be allocated a cash limit and then will have to budget for:
Teaching and non-teaching staff
Goods and services (books, equipment, stationery, etc.)
School cleaning
Caretaking
Building repairs and maintenance
Grounds maintenance
Supporting services (those for whom the client is the school as opposed to the LEA)
Contingencies – unforeseen expenditure.

The governing bodies will need to:
Manage
Plan and budget
Control finance
Manage Information
Administer.

The LEA will monitor schools' management of their budgets and will ask them to account for their achievements and the use of resources. If the LEA thinks the Governing Body is mismanaging its budget, it may take away the Governing Body's right.

The Governing Body may delegate its financial tasks to the headteacher, or select a sub-committee to handle them.

SEE ALSO LOCAL MANAGEMENT OF SCHOOLS (STAFFING) on page 44 and (PREMISES) on page 49.

2. THE CURRICULUM

The curriculum consists of all the learning experiences provided by the school. This includes not only lessons on the timetable and out-of-school activities, but also relationships, behaviour and the general atmosphere, sometimes referred to as the 'hidden' curriculum.

Under the 1986 Education Act the LEA is required to provide every governing body with its statement of curriculum policy.

The Governing Body of a **county**, **voluntary controlled** or **special** school must consider:—

a) The LEA curriculum policy statement

b) The aims of the curriculum in the school

c) How (if at all) the LEA's policy statement should be modified in relation to the school

The Governing Body must also consider separately:

a) Whether sex education should form part of the school curriculum

b) The content and organisation of a sex education curriculum in the school

c) The preparation of a statement if it decides sex education should *not* form part of the curriculum

In all these curriculum matters it is the duty of the Governing Body:

a) To consult the headteacher

b) To consider any representations from the police or people in the community served by the school

c) To consult the LEA when varying the LEA's policy

d) To provide the headteacher and the LEA with any statement required under the 1986 Act (e.g. if sex education is not to be given).

In **voluntary aided** and **special agreement** schools the governors are responsible for the content of the secular curriculum but must take account of the LEA's policy statement. They must delegate to the Head the responsibility for determining and organising the curriculum and ensuring that it is followed within the school.
The same provisions are made about the community and the police, but aided and special agreement governors have no separate responsibility for sex education.

The National Curriculum

The 1988 Education Act sets out the general purposes of the school curriculum and the establishment of a National Curriculum.

Governors share responsibility with the LEA and the headteacher for ensuring that:

- The school curriculum is broad and balanced and meets the requirements of the National Curriculum

- The school curriculum promotes the spiritual, moral cultural, mental and physical development of the pupils at school, and prepares pupils for the opportunities, responsibilities and experiences of adult life

- Courses leading to public examinations for pupils of compulsory school age are for approved qualifications and follow approved syllabuses

- The law on religious education and collective worship is complied with

- Information about the curriculum and pupils' achievements is available to parents and others

The National Curriculum consists of:

1. Core subjects – mathematics, English, science

2. Other foundation subjects – history, geography, tech-
    nology, music, art, physical education and (for second-
    ary pupils) a modern foreign language. Religious educa-
    tion is also included as a foundation subject.

The difference between core and other foundation subjects is that the core subjects will follow more detailed national
programmes. Children will be graded at ages 7, 11, 14 and 16.
They will face formal tests at these ages, but much of the
assessment will be based on class teachers' judgements.
Parents will be given results for their own children and the
authority will publish the results of all the schools. (There is
no legal requirement to publish the results for seven-year-
olds.)

The amount of time to be spent on studying the core and
foundation subjects will not be laid down by law but it is
suggested they should take up about 70% of the week. Schools
will therefore have scope to offer other subjects (e.g. home
economics) in the remaining time available. Governors will be
able to help the Head to decide what these other subjects
should be.

Courses and Examinations

GCSE (The General Certificate of Secondary Education)
is the new single system of examination for pupils at 16+.

7 Grades may be awarded A B C D E F G.
Grade C compares to the former 'O' level grade C and
CSE grade 1.

Most subjects will have a choice of papers or questions to
suit pupils' abilities.
There are one-year GCSE mature examinations for those
over 16.

'A' (Advanced) levels

More academically able students will take two, three or even four 'A' levels which are an entry requirement for Higher Education and many professional posts.

AS levels (Advanced Supplementary)

A new examination for 1989 to give breadth for those following Advanced (A) level courses. AS levels take half the time of an 'A' level and are graded as 'A' levels.

CPVE (Certificate of Pre-Vocational Education)

Post-16 qualification for those not taking 'A' levels. It is a one-year course taught at schools and further education colleges.

RSA (Royal Society of Arts)

Courses cover qualifications in office practice, commercial information and technology skills and also in languages. Examinations are at three stages.

CGLI (City and Guilds of London Institute)

Courses beginning at 4th year level in schools to develop skills for working life.

TVEI (Technical and Vocational Education Initiative)

A government-funded scheme to provide technical and vocational education for 14–18 year olds.

PEI (Pitmans Examination Institute)

Courses and examinations for commercial subjects and languages.

3. THE PUPILS

1. Admission

Arrangements for the admission of children to schools are regulated by the 1980, 1986 and 1988 Education Acts.

The two earlier Acts require each LEA to consult with the governing bodies of schools concerning admission procedures and numbers, and to publish the number of pupils to be admitted to each school. Governors have no specific duties in the matter. They can make observations on the Education Committee's proposals but the LEA need not accept them.

The 1988 Education Act states that the level of admissions must be set initially at the school's "standard number", which is either the number of pupils admitted in 1979 or, if the school is newer than that, the number fixed when it came into being. The Governors can challenge this level of admissions first through the LEA and then, if necessary, the Secretary of the State.

Parents have a choice of schools for their children and if they do not get their first choice they may appeal to the LEA.

Special provision is made to protect the denominational interests of **voluntary aided schools**. The Governors may make an agreement with the local authority to accept only a percentage of non-Church pupils.

2. Discipline

Revised procedures for dealing with the exclusion of pupils from school were included in the 1986 Education Act and came into operation for **County** and **maintained special** schools from September 1988. Similar arrangements applied to **voluntary** schools from September 1989.

The Articles of Government state that the overall conduct of the school is under the direction of the Governors, whilst the Head is responsible for internal organisation and management.

Governors are expected, but not required, to give the Head a written statement of the basic framework for discipline in the school and to offer guidance and support on exceptional discipline problems.

Heads must decide on the actual rules for the school and how they will be kept. They are responsible for ensuring that there is self-discipline, a proper regard for authority and an acceptable standard of behaviour.

Occasionally the situation arises when a pupil has to be excluded from school. Headteachers are the only people who have the power to exclude pupils. Depending on the length of time for which a pupil is to be excluded the Head must give certain specific information to specified individuals, as shown below:—

Period of exclusion:	Head must inform parent, or pupil over 18 years of age:	Head must inform LEA & Governing Body:
Up to 5 days in a term	1. of the suspension 2. of the reason 3. of the right to make representation to Governing Body and LEA	——
More than 5 days or during public exam	Ditto	1. of the reasons 2. of the length
Permanent exclusion	Ditto	of the reasons

Any **review** or **appeal** concerning exclusions takes place in two stages.

Stage 1

Type of exclusion:	Governors:	LEA:
Over 5 days in a term	may confirm suspension or order reinstatement	may confirm suspension or order reinstatement
During public examination	Ditto	——
Fixed Period	Ditto	must consult Governors and may order reinstatement
Indefinite Period	Ditto	must consult Governors and may order earlier reinstatement of pupil
Permanent exclusion	Ditto	must consult Governors and may reinstate pupil

Stage 2

1. The parent (or pupil if over 18 years of age), may appeal against a decision not to reinstate.

2. The Governors have seven days to appeal against an LEA decision to order reinstatement.

This summary is only a guide. Any governor who has to act in any case of exclusion must refer to the Articles of Government where it is stated exactly what has to be done.

The procedures for the exclusion of pupils from **voluntary aided** schools are essentially the same except that the LEA does not have the power to direct the headteacher to reinstate a pupil who has been permanently excluded, and the parents' right of appeal is to the Diocesan Education Authority.

3 Special Needs

Governors must take account of the terms of the 1981 Education Act which deals with children with special educational needs being accepted into ordinary schools.

'Special Needs' refer to learning difficulties which are significantly greater than those of the majority of children of the same age. It has been estimated that 20% of children are likely to have special needs at some time during their school life. Most will receive education in ordinary schools but some will attend special schools or units.

It is the duty of the governing body to ensure that:–

    (i) pupils with special educational needs receive the special educational provision they require

    (ii) the needs of these pupils are made known to all who teach them

    (iii) teachers are aware of the importance of identifying and providing for pupils who have special needs

    (iv) as far as is practicable, children with special needs take part in the activities of the school together with children who do not have special needs

4 Pupil Support

LEAs provide various support services to help schools in their work, and Governors will find it useful to know what assistance the school can receive when problems arise. The diagram on the next page sets out the main means of support:

Careers Officer

The careers service aims to provide vocational, further and higher education guidance. Careers officers work with the schools careers teachers and are local authority employees.

Education Welfare Officer

Monitors, helps and supports families with attendance and behavioural difficulties.

Educational Psychologist

Will help pupils on a referral basis if they are experiencing learning or behavioural problems.

PUPIL SUPPORT

Home Tuition

May be provided by the local authority if a child is ill or, in extreme cases, excluded from school.

Equal Opportunities

Local authority units exist to monitor education to ensure that all pupils receive the best education, regardless of sex, race or disability.

School Health Services

A preventative service which includes medical examinations, screening of vision and hearing, preventative inoculations and the management of children with special educational needs.

Grants

Available under certain circumstances for school meals, clothing and post - 16 education. Education welfare officer (EWO) will provide details.

Transport

To and from school. LEA has to make suitable arrangements for pupils who do not live within walking distance.

4. STAFFING

A. STAFFING IN NON-LMS SCHOOLS

Under the terms of the 1986 Education Act:

- The appointment and dismissal of all staff at a **county**, **controlled**, **special agreement** or **maintained special** school is under the control of the LEA as the employer.

- The LEA fixes the complement of the teaching and non-teaching staff of the school.

- The complement is all the full-time and part-time teaching and non-teaching staff who work only for that school. It does not include meals staff, lunch-time supervisors and staff who work in other schools as well.

- Governors of **voluntary aided** schools are able to make their own arrangements about the appointment and dismissal of staff.

1. Staff Vacancies

When there is a vacancy in the 'complement' posts, the LEA has three choices:

1. The post is no longer needed
2. The post should be advertised and the candidate recommended by the Governors should be appointed
3. An existing employee of the LEA should be redeployed to fill the post

If the LEA decides to advertise, the advertisement must be placed where it will reach all people who are likely to be interested in the job.

The Governing Body has the duty to interview each applicant as it thinks fit and, where it thinks it is appropriate, recommend for appointment to the post, one of the candidates it has interviewed.

The Governing Body can delegate its powers of selection and interviewing to one or more of its members, to the Head, or to one or more of its members together with the Head.

The Headteacher and any person the LEA nominates (normally an inspector/adviser or Education Officer) have the right to be present for the purpose of giving advice whenever an appointment is discussed or an applicant interviewed.

Here is one example of the likely process of selection, interviewing and appointment of teaching staff other than Headteachers. Practices can vary from LEA to LEA.

1. A job specification is drawn up.
    This consists of:–
    a) a job description – duties and responsibilities
    b) a person specification – knowledge, skills, qualities
    c) a school description – further particulars about the school, drawn up by the LEA

2. The post is advertised both in the national press, usually The Times Educational Supplement, and within the Authority.

3. Applicants are sent a job specification.

4. Many advertisements will attract more applicants than it is possible to interview so it will be necessary to reduce the number of applicants to a long list (if there are a large number of applicants) and then to a short-list. Governing bodies need to be involved in this part of the process, but they may decide to delegate their powers according to the level and type of the appointment. For example, appointments on main professional grade are sometimes delegated to the Headteacher with an officer or an inspector from the LEA.

5. Short-listed candidates are invited for interview.

6. The LEA takes up references for short-listed candidates.

7. Interviews are normally held at the school to give candidates an opportunity of going round the school.

2. The Interview

The interview panel will wish to spend some time before the start of the interviews to discuss what questions should be asked and by whom. The framing of a question is important:
 (i) do not ask questions that require only 'yes' or 'no' for an answer e.g. "Do you agree with school uniform?"
   Rephrase it as:
"What are your views on what pupils should wear at school?"

(ii) do not suggest the 'right' answer e.g. "We believe in spelling tests, do you?"
   Rephrase it as:
"How much importance do you think should be given to spelling in an English essay?"

All questions should be clear, short and relate to the requirements of the job.

It is not usually considered good practice to discuss candidates between interviews. This should only happen after all the candidates have been seen, to help give all candidates a fair chance.

It may be agreed at the end of the interviews to eliminate one or more candidates almost immediately from discussion.

The interview panel should then discuss the strengths and weakness of each of the remaining candidates. Discussion should concentrate on putting a precise value on each candidate's relevant assets. A completed person specification chart can be a useful aid to remembering each candidate's qualities, along with their application form.

It can be helpful to summarise regularly throughout the decision-making process. It may then be possible to eliminate further candidates or recommend an appointment.

If the LEA has a policy of equal opportunities it should always be borne in mind.
Some authorities have a staffing policy that values white, black and men and women's perspectives, and encourages a

balanced teaching force. If any group is under-represented, an individual from such a group could bring a perspective and experience that will be an asset to the school and the Authority.

At some stage references need to be read. In a few authorities these can be read only after the panel has decided on the successful candidate. If the reference does not support the view of the panel, it may be impossible to proceed with the appointment.

The successful candidate may be elected by a formal vote or by the Chair gauging the feeling of the panel. He or she is then recommended to the Authority for appointment.

It is the LEA, as the employer that makes the final decision. There may be technical reasons for the candidate not to be appointed e.g. not qualified or a criminal record.

The unsuccessful candidates may welcome a few words from the inspector/adviser or the Headteacher.

3. Re-Deployment

If the LEA decides not to advertise, but to appoint someone it already employs elsewhere, it must allow the Governors, in consultation with the Head, to draw up a specification for the post which it must take into account when making the appointment.

If the Governors disagree with the LEA's choice, this must be reported to the next Education Committee meeting.

4. Appointment Of Headteachers

The LEA, as the employer, makes the actual appointment of Headteachers, but all aspects of candidates' selection are the responsibility of a selection panel.

The membership of this panel is laid down in the Articles of Government. The members are chosen by the Governors and by the LEA. There must be at least three of each. The selection process will then follow the pattern outlined below.

- The panel should meet as soon as possible after the vacancy has been notified in order to agree the criteria for candidates' suitability. Chief Education Officers/ Directors or their nominees have a right to attend all proceedings of the panel.

- A job description should form the basis of an advertisement which should be placed nationally.

- The panel may examine all the applications received but it is not required to do so. It may prefer to ask the LEA Officers to advise on which applicants best satisfy the selection criteria.

- Taking this advice into account, the panel will choose the short list and interview candidates.

- Good practice is likely to include a preliminary tour of the school for short-listed candidates.

- The panel must try and reach a consensus, and there is no longer a 'casting' vote.

- In **voluntary aided schools** the Governing Body and not the LEA controls the procedure.

5. Suspension And Dismissal Of Staff

Staff management is a shared responsibility between the LEA, the Governing Body and the Headteacher.

When Heads suspend a colleague, they must inform the Governing Body.

Similarly when the Governing Body suspends a member of staff, it must inform the Headteacher.

Both Headteacher and Governing Body must also inform the LEA immediately whenever they use their powers to suspend. Furthermore they must end the suspension if the LEA directs them to do so.

As the LEA is the employer, it alone can terminate the employment of staff. This can be by dismissal or by allowing early retirement. Before taking either course, the LEA must consult both the Governing Body and the Headteacher.

B. STAFFING FOR SCHOOLS WITH FINANCIAL DELEGATION – LMS

The responsibilities for staffing that governors have under a scheme for local management of schools are an integral part of financial delegation.

1. Staffing Levels

Governors must decide within the total resources available how many staff should work at the school.

The LEA does not have the power to set a required complement but it may wish to give advice to governors about staffing levels in line with the school's budget and the delivery of the National Curriculum.

The Governing Body will wish to seek the advice of the Head on staffing levels.

2. Appointments

(i) *Teachers other than Heads and Deputies*
(These regulations do not apply to temporary appointments)

Where a vacancy occurs or is due to occur the Governing Body must:
a) determine a specification for the post in consultation with the Head
b) send a copy of the specification to the LEA

The LEA may nominate for consideration for appointment to the post any person who:–
a) is employed by them or is due to be employed by them
b) appears to them to be qualified to fill the post

The Governing Body may advertise the vacancy at any time after it has sent a specification for the post to the LEA, unless it decides to appoint somebody nominated by the LEA or somebody already employed at the school.

The advertisement must be placed where it will reach all people who are likely to be interested in the job.

The Governing Body will interview each applicant as it thinks fit and, where it decides it is appropriate, will recommend for appointment one of the candidates interviewed.

The LEA must appoint the person recommended unless it is not satisfied that the candidate meets the required staffing qualifications.

If the Governing Body cannot agree on an appointment it must repeat the process but is not obliged to re-advertise.

The Governing Body may delegate its powers to one or more Governors, the Head, or one or more Governors together with the Head.

The Chief Education Officer and the Head are entitled to attend, for the purpose of giving advice, all proceedings of the Governing Body relating to appointments.

(ii) *Heads or Deputy Heads*

To make these appointments the Governing Body will be required: –
a) to advertise the vacancy in such publications circulating in England and Wales as they consider appropriate
b) to appoint a selection panel consisting of at least three Governors

The selection panel will interview applicants for the post as they think fit and, where appropriate, recommend to the Governing Body appointment of one of the applicants interviewed. If their recommendation is approved by the Governing Body, the panel will then recommend the successful applicant to the LEA for appointment.

If the selection panel are unable to agree on a recommended person, or if the Governing Body does not approve their recommendation, the process must start all over again except that there is no obligation to readvertise.

The LEA must appoint the person recommended by the panel unless it is not satisfied that the candidate meets the staff qualifications required for the appointment. If this situation arises the panel must start the process again.

Where the LEA declines to appoint a person recommended by the Governing Body as *acting* head, the Governing Body must recommend another person for appointment, but the whole process need not be repeated.

The Chief Education Officer is entitled to attend relevant meetings of the Governing Body to give advice on the appointment and the Governing Body is under a duty to consider that advice.

For the appointment of a deputy head, the Head is also entitled to attend relevant meetings.

(iii) *Non-teaching staff*

Decisions about the selection for appointment of non-teaching staff rest with the Governing Body, subject to the requirement to consult the Headteacher and, if the post involves working for sixteen hours per week or more at the school, the Chief Education Officer.

3. Pay And Conditions

The number of incentive allowances will be decided by the Governing Body within the framework set down in the School Teachers' Pay and Conditions document. The Governing Body will also decide whether a particular teacher appointed to the school should receive an incentive allowance.

4. Discipline, Grievance, Suspension

Responsibility for disciplinary and grievance procedures rests with the Governing Body. It is the duty of the LEA to take action at a request of the Governing Body resulting from disciplinary procedures.

Both the Governing Body and the Headteacher have the power to suspend on full pay anyone who works at the school, but they must both inform each other and the LEA.

Only the Governing Body may end a suspension.

5. Dismissals

The Governing Body has the responsibility of deciding whether or not someone working at the school should cease to do so.

Before coming to a decision, it must consult with the Head (unless he/she is the person concerned) and the Chief Education Officer, and must afford the person concerned an opportunity of making representations, including oral representations, and of making an appeal.

For a person working solely at the school, the LEA has a duty to issue a dismissal notice within 14 days of the date of notification to the LEA by the Governing Body.

In **voluntary aided schools** taking part in financial delegation schemes, the governors have the power to appoint, suspend and dismiss staff as they think fit.

5. PREMISES

1. Lettings

Under the terms of the 1986 Education Act governors are responsible for the use of their school buildings outside normal school times. These responsibilities are not changed under the 1988 Education Act.

Governors have to approve applications for the letting of school premises, or agree other arrangements for applications to be approved.

Governors must take into account any directions given to them by the LEA. These may include rules about permitted times and types of activities and will refer to such things as security, caretaking and the safeguarding of facilities.

Governors are asked in the Secretary of State's Circular 7/87 "to ensure that the School's facilities are widely available to the community served by the school".

2. Capital expenditure is regulated by allocations from the Department of Education and Science. The final decision on these allocations rests with the LEAs. There are three main categories:

    (a) major works (projects over £120,000)
    (b) minor works (projects of £5,000–£120,000)
    (c) minor improvements (projects under £5,000)

3. Repair and Improvement
(i) *Non-LMS schools*

Governors will want to take an interest in the condition and state of repair of the building. The state of the buildings is a frequent item on the Governing Body agenda and governors will wish to keep the LEA informed about the need for repair and improvement.

It will naturally be important to know something about the allocation of funds for school buildings.

For **routine maintenance** and **improvement** a sum of money is normally allocated to each school for additional, or the replacement and repair of, furniture and equipment.

(ii) *LMS schools*

As explained in the section on 'Finance – Local Management of Schools' (see p.28), schools with a delegated budget will be responsible among other things for repair and maintenance of their buildings.

The LEA will retain ownership of the premises and site, and will continue to have responsibility for their protection and development. Commonly, the LEA as landlord will be responsible for all structural repairs and maintenance, including external decoration. As tenant, the school will be responsible for minor repairs and maintenance, including internal painting, replacing windows and doors, etc.

In **voluntary aided** schools the voluntary body has to provide 15 per cent of the school's running costs. In such schools with **local management schemes** governors will have to budget for building repairs and maintenance (see under Finance p.29).

6. ANNUAL GOVERNORS' REPORT AND PARENTS' MEETING

The 1986 Education Act requires governors of every **county**, **voluntary** and **maintained special** school to produce an annual report for parents.

This is to show, among other things, how the Governors have carried out their responsibilities. It is not meant to be just a general report on the school.

All parents must be sent a copy of the report and be invited to an annual parents' meeting held shortly after it is issued.

The Report

It is the Governors' report to the parents, not the Head's.

It is often most effective when a small sub-committee representing the make-up of the Governing Body does the actual writing. Heads may well make a valuable contribution to this.

The style of the report needs to be clear, without too much detail and free of jargon. Parents have appreciated a short report with additional facts in appendices and it has encouraged them to come to the annual meeting to find out more.

Governors should remember that the report may need to be produced in other languages (DES Circular 8/86) if the school has parents whose first language is not English.

The content is laid down in the Education Act:–

(i) What the Governors have done over the year to carry out their responsibilities

(ii) The name of each Governor; whether they are parent, teacher etc; the date their term of office comes to an end; the name and address of the Chair and the Clerk

(iii) Arrangements for the next election of Parent Governors

(iv) What the LEA spent on the school in the last year and its proposed expenditure for next.
How the governors have spent the money available to them (i.e. on books, equipment, etc.)
How gifts to the school have been used

(v) Examination results (for secondary schools)

(vi) Links with the community

(vii) A note drawing parent's attention to syllabuses and educational provisions made for their children. This need not be lengthy, particularly if parents have had some of the information (e.g. exam results) before.

In addition to the list of items specified by the DES, other matters, perhaps contentious, such as the use of the school premises, can add greater interest to the report and encourage people to attend the meeting.

The presentation of reports must make them attractive enough for parents to want to read them. Coloured paper and a few children's drawings or cartoons liven up the text and stiff covers make the report more presentable.

Above all, though must be given to the layout. Write short, simple sentences, with plenty of spaces between sections. The type should be large enough and bold enough to be easily read.

The Meeting

All parents of registered pupils in the school must be invited. The Governors can invite anyone else they wish.

Most Governors feel the presence of teaching and non-teaching staff is a bonus.

In some cases older pupils in secondary schools have been invited too and this has been welcomed.

The DES Circular advises against inviting the press and the public.

Notice of the meeting should be given well in advance with a reminder two weeks before the date, as required by the Act.

A friendly letter of invitation, separate from the report, has been found to be effective. Some governing bodies add a tear-off reply slip to the letter, with a space for notice of questions for the meeting.

The local press and radio can help with publicity.

Attendance over the country is disappointing, but where there are close links between governors, parents and the school, many more of the parents have attended the annual meeting.

These are a few suggestions which might improve attendance:–

1. To combine the meeting with an event, or variety of events, of an educational and/or social nature.

2. To ask questions in the report, such as:–
    Do you agree with the school uniform? The Governors wish to know your views.

3. To provide a creche.

4.   To serve refreshments.

5.   To make part of the meeting an informal chat with parents.

The date and time of the meeting need to be given careful thought. Is late afternoon better than evening? Are parents on shift work? Are there too many other events taking place at this time? Should the meeting be run twice at different times?

The atmosphere of the meeting is crucial. The following suggestions are all worth consideration:

(i)   name tag labels may help
(ii) the arrangement of chairs in a circle or semi-circles is less formal
(iii) comfortable chairs promote relaxed and productive discussion – can the staff lounge or community room be used?
(iv) a roving microphone is useful (i.e. one than can be taken to members of the audience)

The Chair can set the tone of the meeting. The most effective meetings are those where the Chair is firm, yet flexible and friendly.

A good way to open the meeting is for the Chair to give a short personal introduction and up-date parents on anything that has happened since the report was written.

In some governing bodies, individual Governors take a particular interest in one area of Governors' responsibilities and are then invited by the Chair to speak about their work.

Most Chairs find it a good idea to accept questions at the meeting as well as the written questions received beforehand.

Chairs should not allow discussion on individual staff because of the law of slander and natural justice. Most parents respect this.

Resolutions may be passed by a simple majority vote if at least 20% of the parents of registered pupils at the school are present. Where resolutions are passed they have to be considered by the Governing Body, and the Head and the LEA must be sent copies. Any conclusions have to be included in the next annual report.

At the close of the meeting a word of praise for the school and staff is particularly appreciated.

6
THE ROLE OF A GOVERNOR

IN GENERAL, THE ROLE OF THE GOVERNOR IS TO SUPPORT, INFORM AND INFLUENCE THE SCHOOL. SPECIFICALLY AS A GOVERNOR YOU SHOULD:

1. Act as a crucial link between the school, the community and the LEA.

2. Ask questions and seek full and accurate answers.

3. Acquire a full understanding of what the school is trying to achieve.

4. Support the school, particularly if you feel it is not getting a fair deal.

5. Defend the school against unwarranted criticism.

6. Press the school to make educational progress.

7. Take part in important decision-making with the advice of the Head and other professionals.

7
THE EFFECTIVE GOVERNOR

IN ORDER TO FULFIL YOUR ROLE AS A GOVERNOR EFFECTIVELY, YOU SHOULD:

1. Give top priority to Governors' meetings, there are not many. To miss one is to risk being out of date.

2. Read the Articles of Government carefully.

3. Find out about the curriculum, especially the syllabus of a subject in which you have an interest.

4. Ask the Head when it is most convenient for you to see the school at work.

5. Try to learn the names of staff and their responsibilities, particularly senior staff with major responsibilities.

6. Find out if parents are generally satisfied with your school and if local residents think well of it. Read about it in the local press and community publications.

7. Be prepared to attend school functions, fêtes, concerts, presentation days, open days etc.

8. Keep yourself fully informed about training opportunities for Governors and take part in as many as possible.

9. Keep up-to-date on educational legislation and developments

10. Write letters of praise or other comment. All schools welcome feedback.

11. Be discreet about the information you receive as a Governor. Some of it is sensitive.

12. Never disown in public a decision taken by the Governing Body.

13. Never agree to speak on behalf of the Governing Body unless specifically authorised to do so. All public statements are normally made by the Chair or, if not available, the Vice-Chair.

8
PREPARING FOR A GOVERNORS' MEETING

1. Find out:

   a) The date, time and place of the next meeting

   b) Who to contact if you cannot attend

   c) Who to contact if you have not received an agenda

   d) The telephone number of these contacts.

IF IN DOUBT YOU CAN ALWAYS TELEPHONE THE SCHOOL TO ASK FOR INFORMATION OR FOR THEM TO PASS ON A MESSAGE.

2. Read through the agenda papers, making notes in the margin if you wish to query something or make a comment at the meeting.

3. Do not be afraid to ask questions before or during the meeting.

4. ANY GOVERNOR MAY REQUEST AN ITEM TO BE PUT ON THE AGENDA, WITH PROPER NOTICE AS DEFINED IN THE INSTRUMENT OF GOVERNMENT.

5. Be prepared for the election of the Chair. It will come at the beginning of the meeting and often the election is over before new Governors realise it.
    Any Governor, other than a member of the school's staff, can be elected as Chair.

6. Some groups of Governors hold pre-meetings. Parent Governors are quite entitled to do the same.

7. Do not be surprised if you feel inexperienced and a bit confused. There will be others feeling the same.

9
THE GOVERNORS' MEETING

BRING YOUR AGENDA PAPERS

A. TYPICAL AGENDA

1. Appointment
   of Chair

   } Elected annually.

2. Appointment
   of Vice-Chair

3. Apologies for
   Absence

   – Three consecutive absences could lead to disqualification.

4. Minutes

   – Signed by Chair. They should be a formal record of attendance, items discussed and resolutions.

5. Matters Arising

   – Brief reports on action taken given by Chair, Head or Clerk. Opportunity for Governors to raise queries.

6.	Head's Report	– Will outline changes since last meeting, highlight problems, links with parents/community, achievement by pupil(s), school activities, future plans.
7.	Director's or CEO's report	– Will give information on resolutions and requests from LEA, and new legislation and circulars from Central Govt. Will also contain advice and reminders for Governors.
8.	Staffing	– Confirmation of appointments and resignations.
9.	School Attendance	– Statistics provided by school.
10.	Finance	– Reports on, or discussion of, financial matters.
11.	(Possible item from a Governor)	– Any Governor may request an item to be put on the agenda, with proper notice (Check what this is with the Instrument of Government).
12.	Date of next meeting	

B. POINTS OF PROCEDURE

1. All discussion is through the Chair.

2. Decision-making should be thorough and, wherever necessary, reached by majority decision.

3. Voting is not common but where it takes place it is usually by show of hands. The Governors can, however, ask for a paper vote.

4. Each Governor has one vote and the Chair has an extra (or casting) vote if there is a tie.

5. Matters arising from the minutes are dealt with immediately after the acceptance of the minutes and cannot be referred to later in the meeting.

6. Reports are not usually read line by line.
    The Head will highlight important issues in his/her report for the Governors' attention.
    The CEO/Director's report and other reports are usually taken page by page or section by section. Governors who wish to comment or ask questions are expected to do so at the relevant page or section.
    For these reasons, it is vital to have read these reports beforehand so that you are well prepared.

7. 'Any Other Business' is not allowed as an agenda item in many Authorities.

8. Dates and times of meetings are often agreed for a whole year in advance. Remember to bring your diary and watch out for clashes with other meetings and events.

9. Any Governor can put a motion to the meeting. It must be clear, concise and precise. After any discussion on it, the Clerk should read out the motion and once it has been proposed and seconded, it becomes the property of the meeting.
    Before voting takes place, amendments may be put.

These may be a change of words or an omission of a word or words.

If the amendment is proposed and seconded, it is voted on before the original motion.

If it is defeated then the original motion is voted on.

A motion adopted by the meeting becomes a resolution and is binding on all the Governors.

10. Points of order at Governors' meetings are usually: irrelevance, incorrect procedure or 'ultra vires' (against the rules). An example of ultra vires is if Governors were to suggest an extra day's holiday when there are strict rules about the number of days a school may close.

C. FEATURES OF GOOD AND BAD MEETINGS

GOOD

1. Warm, well-lit room with refreshments

2. Punctuality

3. Chair in control/discussion through Chair

4. Report and papers available

5. Preparation by Governors

6. Relevant discussion – clear decisions/resolutions

BAD

1. Cold, ill-lit room – no refreshments

2. Unpunctual members

3. Chair not in control

4. Items taken out of order

5. Private discussions/arguments

6. Time wasting – too much attention to trivia

10
SUMMARY OF THE 1986 EDUCATION ACT

This is a summary of the main points of the Act. Since the language of this summary is intended for quick reading, it lacks the legal accuracy of the text of the Act, to which Governors are advised to refer for more detailed information. (To make this task easier, the numbers of the relevant Sections of the Act are given in brackets in this guide).

Governors should be aware that the 1986 Act builds on, or modifies legislation passed in 1944, 1980, 1981. The Government's intention in passing the 1986 Education Act was to strengthen and be more specific about the powers of governing bodies, Heads and LEAs, and to change the way in which governing bodies are made up. The Government took on many of the recommendations of the 1977 Taylor Report, 'A new Partnership for our Schools', the task of which was to look at the governing of schools.

FINANCE (29)

Governors must decide whether expenditure in their school is an economic, effective, and efficient use of resources.

Governors will have an annual sum to spend on books, equipment and stationery, provided that the Head thinks these are appropriate for the curriculum and the spending complies with LEA conditions.

Governors may delegate the spending of this money to the Head.

The LEA must provide an annual statement of expenditures by the LEA on the cost of running the school, covering both day-to-day and capital expenditure.

REPORTS AND MEETINGS (30 and 31)

Governors must produce an **annual report** on their work, in other languages if appropriate, to be issued free to all parents at least two weeks before the annual meeting. A copy of the report should be given to all persons employed at the school.

The report should be as brief as is consistent with the requirement that it must include:

   (i) Summary of how the Governors have discharged their functions;

  (ii) Details of Annual Meeting, place time etc;

 (iii) Name and address of Chair and Clerk;

 (iv) Names of all Governors together with their category (Parent/LEA/Teacher), by whom they were appointed and the date of the end of their term of office (four year terms as of September 1988);

  (v) Outline of the consideration given to any resolution passed at the previous meeting;

 (vi) Arrangements for parents' elections;

 (vii) Financial statement of LEA's expenditure on the school;

(viii) Financial statement on how the Governors have spent their portion of the monies, plus details of the use made of any gifts;

 (ix) Information on examinations in secondary schools (i.e. as set out in school prospectus);

  (x) Description of what the school has done to strengthen its links with the community and the police;

 (xi) Indications of where information is available on the curriculum (20).

- Governors must hold an **annual parents meeting** to discuss the report, and the way in which the Governors have fulfilled their duties.
- A number of parents equal to 20% of the number of registered pupils is required for the meeting to pass resolutions.

- Attendance at the meeting is restricted to parents of pupils on roll at the school, the Head, members of the Governing Body, together with persons whom they may decide to invite, which may include the teaching and non-teaching staff, and will probably include the CEO/Director or representative. It is advisable that Governors agree on a simple system for monitoring attendance at the meeting.

The LEA has the power to make its own definition of what a 'parent' is (House of Lords decision, 2nd February, 1988) but, in general, a 'parent' is interpreted as someone having responsibility for, or duty to, a child at the school. Parents are comprised of three main categories:

(i) Natural parents (whether or not living with the child)
(ii) Natural parents' partners living with the child
(iii) Persons having legal or actual custody of the child.

COMPOSITION OF THE GOVERNING BODY (3 and 4) from September 1988 (for **voluntary aided** schools from September 1989). See composition chart in Chapter 4, The Governing Body.

There is no provision for non-teaching staff governors. Pupil/student Governors are virtually disallowed by the provision (15) that Governors must be 18 or over on the day of their appointment.

Elections: outline arrangements to be made by the LEA and to be conducted through each school; secret ballot; postal vote if parents wish; Candidates must be 18 + ; all parents must be informed of their right to stand and to vote (5).

Terms of office: 4 years for all Governors, except the Head. Governors can be re-elected/re-coopted (8).

The Head is an ex-officio Governor and, therefore, not subject to the normal term of office. The Head can elect not to be a Governor (4).

Co-opted governors: in selecting co-optees, Governors should have regard to "the extent to which they and the other Governors are members of the local business community". They can only be co-opted by those Governors who have not themselves been so appointed (6).

Removal: Governors can be removed by those who appoint them (8). Where a school has more Governors in a particular category than required and none choose to resign, the Governor who will cease to hold office will be selected according to length of service – the longest serving Governor to be the first to go (14).

DISCIPLINARY POWERS

This section of the Act is extremely complicated. Much of it is designed to avoid repetition of certain cases, (e.g. Governors and LEA disagreeing over the suspension of certain named pupils; teachers refusing to teach them if reinstated). This summary cannot do justice to the original, if you are in need of making active use of it please refer to the Act itself in conjunction with the LEA's own guidelines (23–28).

Corporal punishment is abolished.

Heads shall determine how to promote self-discipline and proper regard to authority amongst pupils, encourage good behaviour by pupils and secure acceptable standards of behaviour. They are also responsible for ensuring that these standards are generally known in the school. Heads have sole power to exclude a pupil (22).

Heads must consult with the LEA if disciplinary standards could lead to increased expenditure (22).

CURRICULUM POWERS (17–21)

LEAs shall:

   (i) determine and keep under review their curriculum policy.

  (ii) make a written statement of curriculum policy to be given to the Governing Body and Head of every school (17).

 (iii) determine dates and times of school terms and length of the school day (21).

Governors:

   (i) shall direct the conduct of the school.

  (ii) must consider what should be the aims of the school's secular curriculum and, in doing so, must take account of the LEA's policy and how it might be modified for their school (18).

In taking these decisions, Governors must consult the Head and the LEA, and take account of representations from community bodies and the chief police officer. They must then furnish a written statement of their conclusions (18).

(iii) must decide if sex education should be part of the curriculum, and make a statement of either their policy regarding its content and organisation, or their conclusions why sex education should not be included (18).

(iv) must provide information to parents on the school's curriculum and educational provision (20).

Heads:

(i) are responsible for the determination and organisation of the secular curriculum and for seeing that it is followed. In doing this they must have regard for the statements of the LEA and the Governors, representations from the community and the chief police officer (18).

(ii) must ensure that sex education curriculum is in accord with Governors' and LEA policy and national legislation (18).

Aided and **Special Agreement Schools**

Governors control content of the curriculum and allocate functions to Heads to enable them to organise and determine the curriculum; as with other schools Governors must have regard to the LEA's curriculum policy (19). They have no separate responsibility for sex education.

APPOINTMENT AND DISMISSAL OF STAFF

LEAs:

(i) shall determine the school's complement of teaching and non-teaching posts (34).

(ii) shall control appointment and dismissal of all staff (35, 41).

(iii) shall appoint a specified number of LEA representatives (not less than three) to be a selection panel (36) for the appointment of Headteachers.

(iv) must consult Governors over the appointments of Acting Heads (37,b).

(v) where vacancies arise for other posts, must decide whether or not to retain the post (38,a).

(vi) shall appoint a Clerk to the Governing Body (40,1) and consult the Governors over that person's appointment/dismissal.

(vii) must consult Governors over staff dismissals (41).

Governors:

(i) shall appoint a specified number of Governors (not less than three) to selection panels for Heads and Deputies (36).

(ii) must be consulted by the LEA concerning the appointment of Acting Heads (37).

(iii) shall interview applicants for other posts and recommend to the authority which candidate to appoint (38).

(iv) shall be consulted over the appointment of Clerk to the Governing Body (40,1) and that person's dismissal (40).

(v) can suspend staff if they feel that exclusion from school is required; but must end the suspension if the LEA so directs (41).

(vi) can recommend to the LEA that a staff member should cease to work at the school (41).

Heads:

    (i) If not members of the selection panel for Deputy Heads, Heads can be present to advise during selection, and must be consulted by the selection panel (39).

    (ii) can suspend staff if they feel exclusion from school is required (41).

    (iii) must end staff suspension if the LEA directs (41).

OTHER MATTERS

    (i) Governors control the use of school premises outside school hours, subject to LEA direction.

    (ii) LEA, Governors and Heads shall forbid:
        – pursuit of partisan political activities by junior pupils (44).
        – promotion and teaching of partisan political views.
    A balanced presentation of political view must be given in any political issue (44 and 45).

    (iii) Sex education shall have due regard to moral considerations and the value of family life (46).

    (v) Secretary of State may require the regular appraisal of teachers (49).

    (vi) In deciding whether or not pupils are entitled to free transport, regard must be made to the pupils' ages, and to the nature of the route (53).

11
SUMMARY OF 1988 EDUCATION ACT

Governors will be given important new powers and duties concerning:

THE CURRICULUM
ADMISSION OF PUPILS
SCHOOL FINANCE AND STAFF
GRANT-MAINTAINED STATUS
(The figures in brackets refer to the sections of the Act)

1. **THE CURRICULUM** (1–8)

    (i) must promote the development of the pupil and society.

    (ii) must prepare pupils for adult life.

    (iii) must be broad, balanced and bear (i) and (ii) above in mind.

    (iv) a common curriculum, to be known as The National Curriculum, must be offered to pupils of compulsory school age.

(v) The National Curriculum will consist of:
core subjects: Maths, English, Science,
other Foundation subjects: History, Geography, Technology, Music, Art, Physical Education and (for Secondary pupils) a Modern Foreign Language. Religious Education is also a Foundation Subject.

(vi) in respect of each of these subjects there are to be attainment targets, programmes of study and assessment arrangements.

(vii) The National Curriculum Council will keep the school curriculum under review.

(viii) there may be modifications of the National curriculum in particular circumstances (e.g. pupils with special needs).

(ix) only external qualifications approved by the Secretary of State may be offered to pupils of compulsory school age.

(x) the requirements of the 1944 Act in respect of religious education must be adhered to.

(xi) pupils will be tested when the majority in the class reach 7, 11, 14, and 16.

2. ADMISSION OF PUPILS TO SCHOOLS (26–32)

(i) the upper limit for admissions will be at the level of the physical capacity of the school.

(ii) the limit will be set initially according to the school's "standard number".

(iii) the "standard number" is either the number of pupils admitted in 1979; or, if the school is newer than that, the number fixed when it came into being; or, if it is higher, the number admitted to the school when the Act came into force.

(iv) if the school can no longer physically take the standard number it can ask the Secretary of State to agree a lower number.

(v) if the Governors think the school can admit a higher number, they may seek a higher limit, first through the LEA and then, if necessary, from the Secretary of State.

(vi) admission numbers must be kept under review.

3. SCHOOL FINANCE AND STAFFING

Finance (33–43)

It is likely that all secondary schools and the bigger primary schools (over 200 pupils) will have responsibility for their own budgets by 1991. To take account of this the LEA must determine each year:

a) the sum of money it needs to keep centrally for such things as capital expenditure, inspectors, educational psychologists, contingencies, etc.

b) the sum of money it will make available overall for schools (the aggregated school expenditure).

c) the means it will use to share out fairly the aggregated money to individual schools.

This sharing out must be done by means of a formula which allows, among other things, for differences in the number age of pupils. The LEA's scheme for doing this must be submitted to the Secretary of State for approval. The school will be allocated a cash limit and will have to budget within that limit for:
– Teaching and non-teaching staff
– Goods and services (books, stationery, equipment, etc.)
– School cleaning
– Caretaking
– Building repairs and maintenance
– Grounds maintenance
– Supporting services (those for whom the client is the school and not the LEA)
– Contingencies (unforeseen expenditure)

The LEA will monitor schools' management of their budgets and will ask them to account for their achievements and use of resources. If the LEA thinks the Governing Body is mismanaging the budget, it may take away the Governing Body's right.

The Governing Body may delegate its financial responsibilities to the Head.

Staffing (44–47)

The Governors will have greatly increased powers in respect of staff appointments, suspensions and dismissals.

When selecting a new Head of Deputy, governing bodies will have to set up a formal selection panel and advertise nationally.

Governors may delegate their responsibility for selecting other staff to one or more Governors and/or the Head.

In relation to the selection of teaching staff governing bodies must consider advice offered them by the Chief Education Officer and the Head who have the right to attend relevant meetings and offer advice.

When selecting staff, other than a Head or Deputy, governing bodies must include, among those they consider, teachers whose names have been put forward by the LEA.

4. **GRANT-MAINTAINED SCHOOLS** (52–99)

The Governing Body of any **county** or **voluntary secondary** school, or any such primary of over 300 pupils, may resolve to initiate procedures leading to an application to the Secretary of State for grant-maintained status.

Parents may make a request for grant-maintained status to the Governing Body. This must be in written form and signed by a number of parents equal to at least 20% of the registered pupils.

Once the Governing Body has passed such a resolution or received such a request, it must notify the LEA.

A ballot of parents must also be held within three months of the resolution or written request, and must be a secret, postal ballot. The arrangements for the ballot will be the responsibility of the Governing Body who will be able to seek re-imbursement for part or all of the costs from the Secretary of State.

If the ballot shows the majority of parents in favour, the Governing Body must, within 6 months, publish its

proposals for acquiring grant-maintained status. These proposals will have to contain specific information about:
a) the existing school
b) the proposed school and its governing body
c) the way in which objections to the proposal may be submitted

After 2 months during which objections may be submitted, proposals will be considered by the Secretary of State who may reject them, approve them, or after consultation with the Governing Body, approve them with modifications.

If a school's proposal for grant-maintained status coincides with a proposal by the LEA under Sections 12 and 13 of the Education Act 1980 (closing or significantly changing a school), the Secretary of State will consider both proposals together but make a decision on the grant-maintained status first.

If the Secretary of State approves a proposal for grant-maintained status, he will make an Instrument and Articles of Government.

The new Governing Body will consist of:

5 elected parents

1 or 2 elected teachers

The Head

A sufficient number of 'first', or foundation Governors, to outnumber the others (at least two of these must be parents). The Secretary of State has the power to appoint two of the 'first' or foundation Governors if the Governing Body is unable or unwilling to do so

2 additional Governors to be appointed by the Secretary of State if the governing body appears to be failing to manage the school satisfactorily

On the date on which approved proposals are implemented:–
i)   the premises will transfer from the former maintaining Authority to the Governing Body
ii) staff employed at the school will transfer without any break of service

During the period of the procedures, the maintaining Authority will be prohibited from disposing of any of the school's assets without the consent of the Governing Body or

Secretary of State. It will also be prohibited from appointing or dismissing staff without the governing body's agreement.

The school must be of the same character as before or, if the Governors wish to change the character of the school or enlarge the premises significantly, they must publish statutory proposals.

The Governors will not be empowered to borrow money and will be required to obtain the Secretary of State's consent before disposing of any of the school's assets.

The Secretary of State will be required to pay the Governors an annual maintenance grant.

The Secretary of State will be able to require an LEA to make payments to him for the school which it formerly maintained

If the Governing Body wishes to discontinue the grant-maintained status, it will be required to publish proposals, to which objections may be made.

If the Secretary of State wishes to discontinue the school, he may do so by giving not less than 5 years' notice to the governing body after long consultation with both it and the LEA. He may give shorter notice if he is satisfied the school is no longer educationally or financially viable. He may then make grants to discharge any debts, liabilities or other costs of winding up the school.

5.   **COLLECTIVE WORSHIP** (6 and 7)

> All pupils in maintained schools are required to attend an act of collective worship in each school day, unless withdrawn at their parents' request.
>
> Headteachers, after consultation with the Governors, can provide for either a single act of worship or separate acts for groups of pupils, held at any time during the school day.
>
> Collective worship in maintained county schools must be non-denominational and must be wholly or mainly of a broadly Christian character. If a school believes Christian worship is inappropriate, the Head may apply to the LEA's Standing Advisory Council for Religious Education (SACRE) for a decision (11 and 12).

6.   **CITY TECHNOLOGY COLLEGES** (105)

   – The Secretary of State will be able to enter into long-
     term agreements for the funding of city technology
     colleges.
   – Capital costs will be shared between the Secretary of
     State and the bodies responsible for running the city
     technology colleges.
   – Normal school running costs will be met entirely by
     the Secretary of State.
   – Costs will be based on the number of pupils recruited.
   – City technology college bodies will be bound by
     undertakings to run colleges in line with conditions
     and requirements laid down by the Secretary of State.
   – City technology college bodies will be accountable for
     grants they receive and for capital assets.
   – City technology college bodies will be indemnified
     against expenditure incurred in termination of the
     agreement.

7.   **ILEA** (162–183)

   – The responsibility for education in the area of an inner
     London Borough or the City of London will be trans-
     ferred from the Inner London Education Authority
     (ILEA) to the council of that borough (or the common
     council of the City of London).

12
GLOSSARY OF EDUCATIONAL TERMS

ACC

Association of County Councils

ACE

Advisory Centre for Education

ADMISSIONS

Normally means the admission to primary school of children in their 5th year of age or of pupils to secondary school at 11 + . It may, however, mean transfer between schools

ADMISSIONS APPEALS

When a child is refused admission to a school an appeal may be made by the parent to the appeal body of the LEA

ADVISER

A member of staff of the Education Department who is an experienced teacher appointed to give general or subject advice to schools. Sometimes advisers are called inspectors (SEE INSPECTORS)

AEO

Assistant Education Officer
Area Education Officer

AGGREGATED SCHOOLS BUDGET	The sum of money the LEA has available to distribute to schools after it has deducted what it requires to spend centrally
AGIT	Action for Governors Information and Training
AGREED SYLLABUS	A non-denominational syllabus of Religious Education used in county and controlled schools drawn up by the LEA
AMA	Association of Metropolitan Authorities
AMMA	Assistant Masters and Mistresses Association
ANCILLARY STAFF	The non-teaching staff of a school
ANNUAL AUDIT	The checking and certifying as correct of financial accounts
AS	Advanced Supplementary Level Examinations
AVA	Audio-Visual Aids
BANDING	The allocation of pupils into broad groups of roughly the same ability
B.Ed.	Bachelor of Education
BLOCK TIMETABLING	A system of timetabling whereby several teaching groups of the same subject or curriculum area are timetabled at the same time
BETEC	Business and Technician Education Council

BULLOCK REPORT (1975)	This report considered, in relation to schools, all aspects of teaching the use of English including reading, writing and speech
CAPITAL EXPENDITURE	Spending on building projects financed mainly from loans
CAPITATION ALLOWANCE	Money allocated to a school each year to spend on books, stationery and equipment
CAREERS SERVICE	A branch of the education department of the LEA
CASE	Campaign for the Advancement of State Education
CDT	Craft Design Technology
CEO	Chief Education Officer
CHILD GUIDANCE	The service provided by LEAs and staffed by psychologists and social workers. Children are referred by schools or family GPs when they have behavioural or educational problems
CLEA	Council of Local Education Authorities
COCKCROFT REPORT (1981)	Considered the teaching of mathematics in schools
COMMUNITY LANGUAGE	A language spoken by a community e.g. Urdu, Punjabi, Polish. Sometimes referred to as 'mother-tongue'
COMPLEMENT	A term used to include all the teaching and non-teaching staff of a school who work only in that school

COMPULSORY SCHOOL AGE	From the term following a child's 5th birthday until one of two dates after the child's 16th birthday. Those reaching 16 before 1st February may leave at Easter; those reaching sixteen from the 1st February may leave in May
COUNTY AND CONTROLLED SCHOOLS	Schools established, owned and maintained by the LEA
CPVE	Certificate of Pre-Vocational Education
CTC	City Technology College
DEO	Deputy or District Education Officer
DES	Department of Education and Science
DISRUPTIVE PUPIL	A pupil considered uncontrollable in an ordinary class
DLO	Direct Labour Organisation
DOE	Department of the Environment
DTI	Department of Trade and Industry
DUAL USE	Premises used by the school during the day and the general public in the evening, at weekends and during school holidays
EMIE	Education Management Information Exchange Service
ESG	Education Support Grant
ESL or E2L	English as a second language

ETHOS	General character purpose and atmosphere of a school
EWO	Educational Welfare Officer
EXCLUSION	When a pupil is either temporarily kept out of school or is permanently removed from the register
FALLING ROLLS	The reduction in school population caused largely by a drop in the birthrate
FE	Further Education It can also mean: Forms of Entry. The size of a school is identified by the number of pupils it admits each year. In a secondary school it is calculated that a form consists of 30 pupils and in a Primary School 35 pupils. Thus a 4FE secondary school is one that admits 4 × 30 pupils
FHE	Further and Higher Education
FIRST SCHOOL	Schools that cater for children aged 5–8 years or 5–9 years
FORM 7	A DES form sent to every school each January. The form provides the DES with a great deal of statistical information on schools and children
FTE	Full-time equivalent Part-time staff may be counted as a fraction of an employee
GCSE	General Certificate of Secondary Education
GMS	Grant maintained school
GRIST	Grant Related Inservice Training

GROUP	Every school is given a group number from 1–14 according to its size. This is determined by the number of pupils on roll multiplied by a weighting factor which increases with the age of the pupil. A very small school of young children will be Group 1 whereas a large secondary school will be Group 10 or above. The group number is reviewed every three years (see TRIENNIAL REVIEW)
HARGREAVES REPORT (1984)	Considered the curriculum and organisation of ILEA secondary schools with special reference to pupils who were under-achieving
HE	Higher Education or Home Economics
HMI	Her Majesty's Inspector
HOD	Head of Department
HOF	Head of Faculty
HOUGHTON REPORT (1974)	Examined the pay of teachers and recommended an average increase of 30%
HUMANITIES	Subjects dealing with human beings and their achievements e.g. history, geography, religion
INCENTIVE ALLOWANCES	Additional salary payments to teachers above the Main Professional Grade
INSET	Inservice Training Courses for teachers wishing to develop and update their professional skills

INSPECTOR	A member of staff of the LEA appointed to give general or subject advice to schools and inspect and report on the work of schools, colleges and teachers
INTEGRATED DAY	A school day not split into periods for teaching purposes but based on the flow of children's interests from one activity to another
IT	Information Technology
JAMES REPORT (1972)	Considered the existing arrangements for the education, training and probation of teachers
LEA	Local Education Authority
LEATGS	System of grants from the DES to support in-service training of teachers
LFM	Local Finance Management
LINK COURSE	A part-time course for school pupils which takes place partly or entirely in the college
LMS	Local Management of Schools
MAIN PROFESSIONAL GRADE	The basic salary of school teachers
MAINTAINED SCHOOLS	Schools supported financially by the LEA. They include county and voluntary schools
MIDDLE SCHOOLS	A school catering for children from 8–12 or 9–13 years

MIXED ABILITY	A teaching group in which children of differing abilities are taught together
NAGM	National Association of Governors and Managers
NAHT	National Association of Head Teachers
NALGO	National Association of Local Government Officers
NAS UWT	National Association of Schoolmasters Union of Women Teachers
NATFHE	National Association of Teachers in Further and Higher Education
NCPTA	National Confederation of Parent Teacher Associations
NFER	National Foundation for Educational Research
NNEB	National Nursery Examining Board
NOR	Number on roll
NUPE	National Union of Public Employees
NUT	National Union of Teachers
OPEN PLAN	A term used to describe schools in which there are large shared teaching areas instead of traditional classrooms
OPTIONS	Subjects chosen by secondary pupils to be studied in the two years before GCSE

OPTING OUT	Schools changing to grant-maintained status
OU	Open University
PA	Parents Association
PASTORAL CARE	The support and care structure within a school. It can be based on either a house or a year system.
PAT	Professional Association of Teachers
PERIPATETIC (TEACHERS)	Employed to teach in a number of schools, usually to give specialist instruction
PGCE	Post-graduate Certificate in Education
PRIMARY SCHOOL	Catering for children in the age range 5–11
PROBATIONARY YEAR	The initial period of service as a qualified teacher is a probationary period usually of one year, during which teachers must show themselves as proficient
PTA	Parent Teacher Association
PTR	Pupil Teacher Ratio. For example a PTR of 19:1 means that the school is entitled to 1 teacher for every 19 pupils
READING AGE	A pupil's ability to read at a given age is tested and compared with the average ability of others of the same age

RECEPTION CLASS	A term sometimes used for the class into which children are received on their first admission to school
RECORDS OF ACHIEVEMENT	This is a concise record of pupils' development and performance throughout their secondary school life and is available to employers when pupils apply for a job
REMEDIAL EDUCATION	Specialist help for individual pupils who have difficulties in certain curriculum areas
RISING 5s	Children are, by law, admitted to school at the beginning of the term following their fifth birthday. During the term in which their fifth birthday falls, the children are known as rising 5s.
SACRE	Standing Advisory Council for Religious Education
SCHOOL ATTENDANCE ORDER	If parents fail in their duty to ensure that their child receives suitable education an LEA can issue such an order requiring the parents to have the child attend a named school
SCIP	Schools Curriculum Industry Partnership
SECONDARY SCHOOL	A school catering for children aged 11 or over
SECONDMENT	A system for releasing teachers to study full time or attend another institution on full pay

SECTION 11 GRANT	The Government provides 75% of the cost of employing extra staff to make special provision for substantial numbers of pupils from the Commonwealth whose language or customs differ from those of the indigenous population
SEO	Society of Education Officers
SETTING	Organisation of pupils into groups according to ability for the teaching of particular subjects. An individual pupil may be in one set for mathematics and another for English, depending on aptitude
SHA	Secondary Heads Association
SIBLING	A brother or sister
SPA SCHOOLS	Social Priority Area Schools where teachers are paid additional allowances for working in an area of high social stress.
SPECIAL AGREEMENT SCHOOLS	These owe their existence to pre-1941 agreements between the Government and voluntary bodies. About 150 special agreement schools were set up under the 1944 Education Act.
SPECIAL SCHOOL	A school providing for children with special educational needs
STREAMING	Pupils divided into different classes according to their ability for all or most of their work
SUPPLY TEACHER	A teacher employed to fill a temporary vacancy caused by the absence of a teacher

SUSPENSION	This occurs when the Headteacher decides a pupil's conduct cannot allow her/him to remain in the school
SWANN REPORT (1985)	This reviewed the educational needs and attainments of children from ethnic minority groups
SYLLABUS	A programme of work in a given subject
TAYLOR REPORT	An inquiry set up in 1975 to review the arrangements for the management and government of schools
TC	Training Commission (This has replaced the Manpower Services Commission)
TEAM TEACHING	A means of school organisation in which a group of teachers work together in the teaching of a large group of pupils, instead of each teacher instructing a smaller group
TEMPORARY CLASSROOM	A classroom normally provide to meet a short-term need. It may also be called a caravan, a terrapin, a mobile classroom, a 'hut' or a relocatable classroom
TRIENNIAL REVIEW	The school's group size (See GROUP) is reviewed every three years. The pupil population is taken from Form 7 and an average taken over three years
TRIST	Technical and Vocational Education Related Inservice Training

TVEI	Technical and Vocational Education Initiative
UBI	Understanding British Industry
UCCA	Universities Central Council for Admissions which acts as a clearing house for dealing with applications for University
UNIT TOTAL	The unit total is determined by the Triennial Review. (See TRIENNIAL REVIEW). From this is calculated the group size of the school
VERTICAL GROUPING	Classes formed with children of different ages
VIREMENT	A system whereby it is permissible to transfer money from one heading to another
VOLUNTARY SCHOOLS	Schools initially provided by bodies other than LEAs e.g. Church Schools
WARNOCK REPORT	This report of 1978 reviewed educational provision for handicapped children in England, Scotland and Wales
WEA	Workers Educational Association
WITHDRAWAL GROUP	A small number of children taken out of normal lessons to be given special tuition
WORK EXPERIENCE	A scheme whereby pupils are taken out to see and experience conditions of work in various branches of industry and commerce
YTS	Youth Training Scheme organised by the Manpower Services Commission.

INDEX